World ISM

Fred Rouady

Publisher: Inspiring Publishers,
P.O. Box 159, Calwell, ACT Australia 2905
Email: publishaspg@gmail.com
http://www.inspiringpublishers.com

TIILINININI A catalogue record for this
book is available from the
NATIONAL
LIBRARY National Library of Australia
OF AUSTRALIA

National Library of Australia Cataloguing-in-Publication entry

Author: Fred Rouady
Title: World ISM
Genre: Political
ISBN: 978-0-6482934-6-0

Contents

Contents

PREFACE

- We're all wanting a good future, for ourselves, our country, our children, our families and most important a better world. But can we trust the current government / politicians to deliver?

- They seem to be more interested in themselves and their political party and have split their nations into 2 groups. LEFT OR RIGHT.

- People feel upset so they don't bother following, what is going on in the world. But what this does is to put people in 2 camps either LEFT or RIGHT parties domestic or internally. But either side does not solve world wide problems it actually continue them. Surely there must be away to solve problems. MIDDLE-ISM for want a better name.

- It won't cost the earth to fix problems, but it will cost the earth one day not to fix problems.

- That's what the book is about. I have the privilege to be able to look deeply into these things. And what i discovered is worth sharing. Worth doing.

- So what can we do to make sure that a good future does happen?

- One thing is for for sure. Its guaranteed that if we continue on the path we're on, then things will go even further downhill. From world wars, religious persecution, bad governments doing evil things to their own people and other nations people, famine, disease, slow response to natural disaster, election fraud, destruction of environment etc. This is a worldwide phenomenon.

- Looking at a third way MIDDLE-ISM. The basic idea that i want to convey is that the solution to some of the world's problem is to find a new way. Citizens of most nations in the last 20 years seem to be following left or right more and more and now it's more of a problem.

- MIDDLE-ISM is the next phase for a peaceful and better world. Its not communism, dictatorship, autocracy it's not socialism, its capitalism. It's the best from all three and the worst parts left out.

- Politicians tend to favour sides, in order to get voted into government and the voters have become like cheerleaders. Blindly Cheering their team even if they agree or disagree thinking there is no other choice. Votes are waiting for the next good thing.

- If we look at things from a historical perspective. Throughout history, the world has gone through different phases. Bronze age, dark ages, colonisation, industrial revolution, capitalism versus communism and the era of technology. All of these have brought about massive changes in how things operate, but have they solve the basic problems that have face mankind. NO.

- Reverse colonialism (refer to chapter 2) reducing military expenditure by 50%, this would go along way towards effecting not just change, but a real solution for every human being.

- This does not put a end to capitalism, the wealth that each country produces is still there, but redirected. Capitalism will actually flourish with MIDDLE-ISM. The money is still spent but on more valuable things, then the wheels of economy will continue to turn because the per capita per spend per person will increase. Because the more worthwhile spending on things that will used, rather than military hardware. It will bring a extra 2 to 3 billion people into the consumer market and the 21st century.

- The world is getting smaller and smaller through technology and fast travel, so we're getting closer to each other, but our thinking seems to be further and further from a global consensus on major topics.

- We need the governments of the world to agree on which 8 key themes which are military expenditure, reverse colonisation, bad governments, religions, supervised elections world wide, respond quicker to natural disasters, environment and a stronger United Nations.

- This organisation is not just about feel good ideas, but a general summary and action plan of each theme.

CHAPTER 1

WORLD MILITARY SPENDING

HISTORY:

The world has spent over 45 trillion US dollars combined on military expenditure since World War 2. Its predicted that the world is going to spend another 31 trillion by 2036 combine. There has been over 45 million people dead including war related deaths and 100 million displaced since World War 2. There have been over 200 million people killed in wars due to lack of healthy, food, water and lack of sanitization all due to overspending on military both in developing & developed world. Even as resent as 2014 there are were 12 conflicts where more than 1000 deaths occurred conflicts is Syria has killed hundreds of thousands. This is not including the other 35 long term conflicts. Still expenditure into defence has not reduced and in the last 15 years R & D into Robotics and Drones wars. When is it going to stop?

LEFT VIEW:

- The world spends to much on weapons
- We don't need a large army to protect us but a sustainable army
- Peace is needed for mankind
- The money can be spent on health, food, water, social services and infrastructure in our country and around the world
- We fear for our soldiers going to war

- My child will end up joining the army and going to war

- Why are we doing military exercise near that country

RIGHT VIEW:

- A military build up is good for our country
- It creates jobs
- It's good for certain towns and cities that have defence bases and factories. Our defence forces are our pride
- We need a army to protect us in case of a war
- Our capabilities are better than their capabilities
- Look at our new military technology
- It is not our problem if we sell military hardware to other countries to kill people
- We need more resources for army veterans
- The children of poorer families will end up joining the army and facing death or injury

LEFT & RIGHT CYCLE:

We have a good military / the other side is catching up / let's spend more on new military technology / the weapons are outdated throw them in the bin.

MIDDLE-ISM SOLUTION:

1. The world needs better co -operation between the top 6 military powers. They need to join together through treaties and stop competing with each others military this goes against human nature and the history of mankind. It usually happens after a war where there is peace

treaty and the winner imposes its ruler against the loser. Let's skip the next major war between the top military countries. The top 6 need to be allies at all time, not only for a better world but for the sake of their own people, who will suffer of any future war between each other. RUSSIA, CHINA AND INDIA NEED TO JOIN NATO. New name EAST WEST NATO. When these countries join forces together plus the 29 other Nato countries then for the first time in world history there will be no major military enemies and reduce terrorist threat amongst the top 6 military nations. WHO WILL STAND UP TO THE LARGEST ARMY IN THE WORLD. This will be the most significant turning point in the history of the world and will guarantee humans survival well into the next century. The threat of major powers at war reduce significantly for the first time in Mankind's history. Only smaller insufficient military countries would exist outside of the new East West NATO alliance.

2.   When there is no more conflict between the top 6 military powers then we can reduce the world military expenditure by 50%. That leaves around $800 billion US dollars a year that can be spent on improving humans world-wide. This may take up to 5 years to implement. To re-train soldiers, re -invent factories, etc. Mass unemployment won't happen, because it takes 5 years to re-deploy the personnel, into more productive activities. There are currently 20 million military personnel worldwide half of those need to learn to work elsewhere in non-military jobs. This all goes against human nature because we were taught from a young age that a strong army protects us but what they haven't told us is that it makes more competition as well.

3.   The top 6 military powers need to have a system in place to monitor each others activities to ensure for no cheating occurs when reducing military spending by 50%. This was done to Germany and Japan who weren't allowed to build their army after WW2 and was closely monitored. This was also done when Russia and USA monitored and reduce each others nuclear weapons.

MIDDLE-ISM SAYING:

1.   Whenever there is a war then usually there a negotiated peace after.

2.   Do the negotiated peace now and save us the hassle of going to war, killing and destruction for all humans. The top 6 military nations join NATO to make it EAST WEST NATO.

3.   When will major war end, another war might destroy the earth. Let's skip the major wars for good.

EXAMPLE 1:

- USA 2016 military budget was $600 billion.

- Reduced spending by 50%,which leaves $300 billion for its own defence.

- $300 billion - 70% = $210 billion for the improvement of the American people.

- $300 billion - 30% =$90 billion for the development and expansion of East West NATO, United Nation and Reverse Colonisation.(please refer to chapter 2).

EXAMPLE 2:

- Total nation military spending $2
- 50% for its own army leaves $1
- $1 is left - 70% to better its own people.
- $1 is left - 30% to NATO army, United Nations and Reverse Colonisation.

MIDDLE-ISM VISION DRAWING:

**CHINESE, AMERICAN, RUSSIA
AND FRENCH SOLDIERS UNITED**

CHAPTER 2
REVERSE COLONISATION

HISTORY:

1. Colonization is a process by which a large country invades directly or indirectly a weaker power to dominates its land and people. Which reduce the poorer nation to not much more, than slaves. This has been occurring since ancient times. In the last 300 to 400 years the main culprits has been European countries including the English and have focused their colonist ways in the Americas, Pacific, Asia and Africa.

2. Modern days colonisation after WW2 include Europe, America, France and Russia, have used politically ideology, resources, military bases and trade for a excuse to colonist and then scale back their colonialism only to find that China has sent millions of their people to these former countries. And in the next 20 years china will continue this trend.

LEFT VIEW:

*   The countries that have been colonist in the past, that are now developed or developing countries like America, Canada, Australia, Tibet and Brazil wants it to be reversed and the current people to leave the lands they have conquered and pay for past crimes against the indigenous people

- They want indigenous people to receive more money, land and subsidised everything
- "WE OWE THEM FOR INVADING THEIR LAND"
- Everything is racism towards the indigenous people
- It was not discovered or explored its was a invasion
- The modern day form of colonisation where the colonize (developing nations and third world) are not able to get ahead because the colonist (developed nation) are exploiting then. The left are demanding their governments to be fairer in trading with smaller third world nation
- A better deal for third world nation resources, their people and a better trading deal
- Better pay and conditions for the workers, where the developed nations buy it goods from third world nations

RIGHT VIEW:

- We shouldn't pay for pass generations actions and crimes
- Only a indirect link between this generation and the pass 4 or 5 generations
- Colonisation was the order of the day back then and if it wasn't a certain country then it would of been another country colonising
- The colonist did the indigenous people a favour by exploring their primitive culture to bring a better modern world
- Modern day Colonization has opened the world to trade and better governments which help people who seek a better life to stay in their countries and in return reduce the number of refugees coming into our country

- Trade has lifted the quality of life in third world nations.
- It may or may not be cruel by exploited another country for our own interest but It does not affect me directly

LEFT & RIGHT CIRCLE:

A stronger country dominates the weaker country / Exploiting begins / they are exploiting us / we need to rule ourselves.

MIDDLEISM SOLUTION:

1. It convenient for community leaders to dwell on the past this needs to stop. Current indigenous population in developed countries have not come to terms with their surroundings and anyone or anything dwell on the past will affect their future. The only way the current indigenous generations can view the past is to learn from the past and in brace the future of the modern world but still keeping their cultural and traditions.

2. The top 25 economic countries need to take a willing third world nation (cousin) under their wing. They need to mentor, training and provide aid to these countries directly. They need to show them how to use their own resources and strength more wisely and reduce selling them military equipment and selling them more goods to benefit their own people.

3. Some developed countries can take on more then just one cousin, some have the resources to take on 3 or 4 cousins. They can help raise the standard of living while respecting their culture and identity unlike the colonist of the pass. This will be known as REVERSE COLONISATION.

4. This also helps the developed and western nations as once the third world nations (cousins) is on its feet and more and more people come out of poverty. In the long run having a self-sufficient country is a good asset for a developed nation as they will end up being consumers to their products they are selling. A perfect example of this is China and India. Since they have lifted the standard of their own people the world's trade has benefited.

MIDDLE-ISM SAYING:

- REVERSE COLONISATION can help over 40 to 50 nations over a 8 to 10 year period. In the space of 15 to 20 years the world can have over 80 to 100 nations better off when implemented right.

- REVERSE COLONISATION means a extra 2 to 3 billion consumers for developed nations. No more third world countries.

MIDDLE-ISM EXAMPLE:

Developed countries	Cousins
1. France	Tunisia, Tanzania, Cape Verde
2. Norway	Angola, Botswana
3. Japan	Myanmar, Cambodia

MIDDLE-ISM VISION DRAWING:

1700's - 1800's

COLONISATION

2000's - 2100's

REVERSE COLONISATION

Dots on maps represent bases

CHAPTER 3

Bad Governments, Serious Nation building

HISTORY:

Bad forms of governments have killed more people in the history of the world then everything else combined since Pharoah time. In the 19 century over 150 million have died due to bad decisions from government and hundreds of millions of people have suffered. Currently there are over 40 to 50 nations who are third world or need help, and another 30 to 40 nations who have bad governments. Bad governments and systems can be in the form of aristocracy, democracy, oligarchy, republic, dictatorship, military, monarchy, communism and socialism. Decent citizens in bad or third world nations are powerless to stop the corruption for a number of reason like being killed or put in jailed or persecuted. Since 1990's nation building has been tried more for political reasons then for right reasons and the countries that object to interference are usually the countries who are sabotaging the good will countries. It's not the land or mountains that is corrupt its the government.

LEFT VIEW:

- It is shocking what is happening on the news all these people dead and not enough food. Wish we can help
- Let us go and do social work and volunteer in their countries. Don't invade these nation

- We caused these problem by invade these nations on the other side of the world
- Why should the United States be the only nation taking a leading role
- It is a imperial ideology. Its for oil and natural resource. That is shocking what is happening in their country
- Let them migrate to our country

RIGHT VIEW:

- It is their problem that nations at war
- Why don't they fix their own country
- The united nation are supposed to deal with war
- Stop sending money to corrupt governments it is going into the wrong hands and it's not filtering down to the people
- They voted for the wrong leader and wrong system
- Don't send our nation army only if we benefit from it
- It's because of religion that this country is at war

LEFT & RIGHT CIRCLE:

Government come to power / corruption starts / people suffer / please help us to stop bad governments

MIDDLEISM SOLUTION:

1. One uniformed and mighty world army is needed to stop bad governments, keeping the peace and implementing United Nation laws. Russia, China and India needs to join Nato and its 29 member countries the new name will be known as East West Nato (refer to chapter 1).

2.   Nato has a number of bases throughout the world and it is already established but needs to expand it bases further in North and south Africa, eastern Asia, Asia and south America.

3.   New agenda will be to stop bad governments or bad leaders from killing people. Last century bad government have killed more people than everything else combined. The sheer present of East West Nato will scare any bad governments not comply with international law. It will stop future wars, future genocide, election fraud and save hundreds of millions people lives. It will reduce corruption and give billions of people hope for a better future. Bad evil governments need to be stopped.

4.   This is only a stage 1 process step 2 reverse colonisation (refer to chapter 4) needs to be implement straight after.

MIDDLE-ISM SAYING.

Stop bad governments the world will improve. There will still be poorer and richer nations but no more third world. Only developing and developed countries.

MIDDLE-ISM VISION DRAWING:

AFRICA COMING OUT OF WAR

CHAPTER 4
RELIGION

HISTORY:

Religion has been around in all different ways for the last 5000 years ever since humans can write. There is currently over 9000 religions. The main religions throughout the word Christianity, Islam, Buddhism, Hinduism and tribal. Most religion has a main focal point (building structure) in the community where people meet to pray and to carry out social services like marriages and funerals.

Religions, religion beliefs and religion clergy have also killed hundreds of millions of people and has made hundreds of millions of refugees in the name of their gods for the last 2000 years.

After WW2 the trend is continuing and no signs of stopping. There has been countless of religious wars in the last 40 years.

Religions groups have worked with bad governments and even instructed their governments to go to war or do evil and weird things to their own people. They have performed rituals before a army going to war to make soldiers believe that gods is on their side. Its has shaped nation boards more than anything else.

A merging factor in not only in third world but developed countries where leaders are running for office usually at the back of religious persecution. Fearing that a particular religion is going to take over.

Currently in the third world or developing countries there is a cold religious war where different religions are living side by side but have segregated community within their own boards.

LEFT VIEW:

- I don't like religion
- Religions start war
- Believe in god but not religions
- The churches only want money
- I only go to my place of worship on holy days like Easter, Christmas, Eid or festival
- Don't really read or understand my religion book it's just too confusing
- I believe in science not god

BOTH LEFT & RIGHT VIEW:

- I believe in god but not religion
- I am a atheist because of religions clergy
- My religion is right yours is wrong
- My religion only seems to be interest in money and property
- I am not a practising worshiper

RIGHT VIEW:

- We are a Christian nation, a muslim nation, etc.
- We only want the same religions in our neighborhood or country

- My fellow worships are my brothers and sisters
- Maybe we should donate more money and time to our place of worship
- Our religion is the best religion and it's a good way to live. We do it god's way and the other religions are wrong
- Without god laws people tend to do bad things
- I have now found god
- I never miss a weekly sermon
- I don't want that religion in my country
- I am atheist because of religion glergy

LEFT & RIGHT CIRCLE:

A child is born / already belongs to a religion / my religion is better than yours / end up persecution people or being persecuted.

MIDDLE-ISM SOLUTION:

1. All religious clergy and politicians present or future has to sign a deed that state killing or persecution people base on a different religious belief or encouraging their follows to do so and is against humanity. No clergy can practise their religion if they don't sign a deed and respect other religions anywhere in the world. This has to be part of the constitution for all countries, religions and United Nation. You simple can't kill people because they are a different religion. United Nations and all countries need to adopt, monitor and enforce this as well.

2. Politicians who get elected have to sign that they will not discriminate against the different religions in their own countries especially if a certain religion is a minority. This

will lead to less war's, less religious persecution, and save hundred of millions of lives and reduce the number of the current 60 million refugees. One of the main reasons for civil wars is due to different religions in one country.

3.   Economic sanctions and united nation funding, public shame for the nations who break or encourage religion persecution within their community. Any religion group in western countries that doesn't follow religion harmony should lose its charitable benefits, and all countries can enforce this.

MIDDLE-ISM SAYING:

One world wide system to monitor all religion and religion glergy. No more killing based on religion beliefs.

MIDDLE-ISM VISION DRAWINGS:

5 MAJOR RELIGION CLERGY AS FRIENDS

CHAPTER 5
ELECTIONS FRAUD WORLDWIDE

HISTORY:

Since ancient times the greeks and romans have used elections to flourish there democracy. The citizens of a country choose who they want to representative then and of course the majority wins. By 1920's women have rights to vote and that spread throughout the world. After WW2 a lot of developing and third world nations still did not allow their citizens to vote due to monarchy, dictation, occupation, war or whenever they did allow elections they would be involved in ballot stuffing, misleading voters on how to vote, voter rigging, intentionally keeping voters line long for hours or close booths early, election fraud and intimidation at polling places and still have the nerve to turn around and claim victory on election day. The blackmailing, intimidation and assaulting of candidates happens in all rich and poor countries. The parties that have committed election fraud always committed further corruption when in governments.

Election fraud is underestimated and overlooked and its the main reason for poverty in the world and it currently effects over 40 nations in the world and numerous of developing nation can't get ahead. When a government comminutes fraud its repeated and repeated for decades.

LEFT VIEW:

- If we win the elections they must be fair, if we lose they have been rigged

- There was no independent parties to witness the elections if it was fair
- We should do something about the process it's unfair for the people

RIGHT VIEW:

- If we win the elections they must be fair if we lose they have been rigged
- In other poor countries people always die during elections
- That country is not really a democracy
- That dictator has been there forever
- Thats is why countries are poor
- We had more votes but a technically gave the win to otherside

LEFT & RIGHT CIRCLE:

Voting day / we wow / the otherside cheated / wait for next elections, system is corrupt.

MIDDLE-ISM SOLUTION:

1. The united nations with the help of East West Nato need to supervise and take control over all elections and the whole process in third world and developing nations. Countries that refuse monitoring on the ground always have something to hide.

2. They should lose United nation support, aid money and their elections not register. The world needs to be there at the begin and not just act after vote fraud occurs. Election

fraud is underestimated and overlooked and its the main reason for poverty in the world and it currently effects over 40 nations in the world and the ability for third world and developing nations to get ahead.

3. This system doesn't apply to the top 30 economies countries in the world. Because there voices are heard and there votes counted, economics sound and stable.

MIDDLE-ISM SAYING:

Election fraud makes the whole nation feel like a jail without committing a crime inside there own country.

MIDDLE-ISM VISION DRAWING:

NO FEAR. A LINE OF PEOPLE QUENING TO VETO

CHAPTER 6
UNITED NATIONS

HISTORY:

United nations was formed in 1945 after WW2 and a replacement for the league of nations. Its aim is to maintaining peace and security, monitor and promote human rights, distribute humanitarian aid and stop conflicts from beginning and act as peacekeepers when the time arises.There are around 193 countries on the planet and all are members.

For the last 2500 years world powers at the height of their powers will rule their corners of the world as they see fit like the Greeks, Romans, Mongols, Ottomans and Europeans countries and make decisions to suit themselves.

After 1945 the top 5 permanent countries France, United States,Russia, United Kingdom and China have the power of veto. Which enables then to say NO to any resolution brought before the council. They have used this privilege for their own interest and the interest of a allie. This has resulted in the united nation to have a mix result when mediate conflicts throughout the world. The Veto powers of the big 5 has slow down decisions on peace and security which has cause the smaller nations to predict the outcome of resolution results.

The world has changed dramatically since the united nations was formed in the 1940's but the system of the united nation has kept almost the same.

LEFT VIEW:

- The united nation need more powers more money more authority
- My government doesn't respect united nations when a decision is not favorable
- Debate of reforms is long overdue over 30 years

RIGHT VIEW:

- Its weak and corrupt. It doesn't stop wars
- Its doesn't support my views so i dont like it
- I don't respect the united nations
- We shouldn't take orders from a less favourable country
- The united nation effectiveness, efficiency and responsiveness to international events are slow

LEFT & RIGHT CIRCLE:

All nations vote democratic for new resolution / it's not in our interest / one permanent member blocks resolution / nothing gets down

MIDDLEISM SOLUTION:

1. All united nation resolutions need to be implemented and enforced.

2. India needs to be a permanent member to make it 6 permanent members.

3. United nation veto powers needs to change where the 5 permanent members plus India which makes it 6

permanent members need 2 vetoes to stand not just the current 1. Unless it's a resolution that directly involving themselves. Abolishing veto is not an option. The 6 permanent members are important because of their large population, military capacity, economic size, influence and contributions.

4. The united nation needs a advance, strong military that can be called upon in time of crises but can never be used against the top 6 permanent members. It will be used for natural disasters, monitoring elections, military conflicts which will result in a better world. East West Nato is its only option. (refer to chapter 1). East West Nato will become the much needed military army for the United Nation and it will give it strength and meaning.

MIDDLE-ISM SAYING:

A modern world organization needs a strong worldwide organization.

MIDDLE-ISM VISION DRAWING:

UNITED NATIONS THE MOST IMPORTANT
ORGANIZATION IN THE WORLD

CHAPTER 7

NATURAL DISASTERS WORLDWIDE

HISTORY:

A major natural disaster is when nature turns on humans it can be a form of bushfire, floods, earthquake, landslide, volcanic eruptions, tsunamis, hurricanes, cyclone etc. Earthquakes and floods are the biggest natural disasters by far. It can cause a great number of deaths and property damage during and after the event. Over the last 2000 years natural disasters have destroy cities like Pompeii, Atlantis and Aleppo. What is left of the population tend to move to another cities. In the last 500 years Asia was experience the most devastating natural disasters, China floods and earthquakes, Indian cyclone and East Asia earthquakes.

In recent times Western countries suffer as much as third world countries. The most occuring natural disaster is the Americas and Asia. Over 60 billion is spent in one year for insurance payouts when major disaster strikes.

Usually every country is on its own at the start and during a natural disasters and than other countries respond but it's too little and often slow. Then the often to little to slow United nation, Charities and governments react with support in the searching stage, relief efforts and aid.

LEFT VIEW:

- So sad that this happen
- Should donate money and our government should donate more money and aid
- Should give then a bigger loan
- Need government help in relief efforts
- Didn't have enough insurance or no insurance for this natural disasters
- My government doesn't care about poor people or the working class. Never good enough

RIGHT VIEW:

- Every country for themselves
- Shouldn't give money to overseas disasters should help the people at home
- Some charities take more money to operate them, then they give out in aid
- Lucky we have insurance
- Thanks to my government for helping

LEFT & RIGHT CIRCLE:

Natural disasters occurs / we need help now / we are coming / to little to slow.

MIDDLE-ISM SOLUTION:

1. Human disease should be called a natural diseases disasters.

2. Need natural disasters bases spread throughout the world for quick response on the ground within 10 hours. 7 major bases need to be in position throughout the world. The bases to be positioned where 90% of the world's population is served quickly. United Nation and East West Nation need to take control of the bases.

3. New bases should be positioned in North America, South America, East Asia, West Asia, Central Africa, Europe and 1 in the Pacific.

4. Need much more Research & development and better equipment and tools to help detect natural disasters and to help during the disasters.

MIDDLE-ISM SAYING:

90% of the world population is served under a 10 hours of flight when disaster occurs.

MIDDLE-ISM VISION DRAWING:

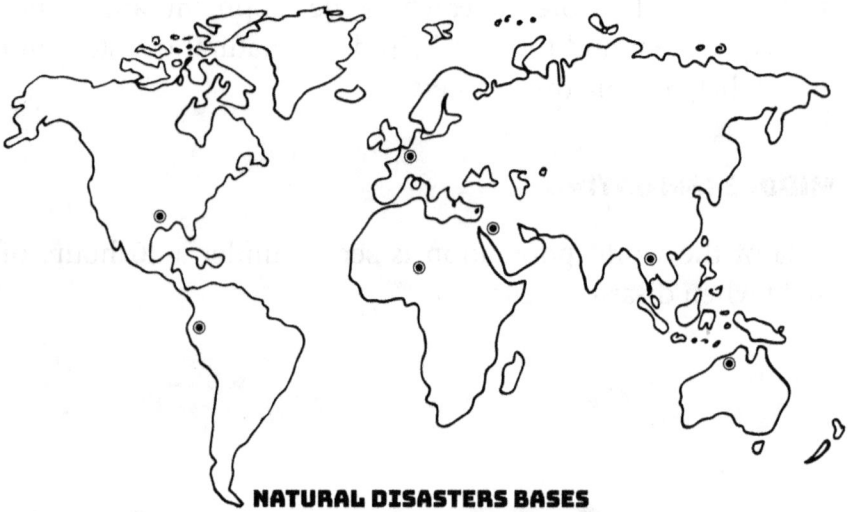

NATURAL DISASTERS BASES

CHAPTER 8

ENVIRONMENT

HISTORY:

The natural environment can be classify as climate change, all forms of pollution, soil, water, air, global warming, logging, animal excition, over mining,etc etc Before the 20th central government and empires has not paid much attention to the environment they did as then please with little or no concern to the environment. In the middle of the century people started to buy ozone generator and were told that ozone contribute to respiratory. In the last 30 years political parties have taking hold of the environment throughout the world and have used it to get vetoes and have over exaggerated the situation, their future predictions on not acting on the environment, have actually turn people away from doing anything for the environment. This has helped the selling of environment goods to skyrocketed.

The protection for the natural environment against human interference has stepped up since the early 1990's. Most people in western countries have mistakenly considered the environment as only global warming, but tend to ignore other environmental issues. Like pollution of our oceans and water systems with plastic waste, over logging, etc. The earth has turned on humans lately with massive typhoons in Asia, Hurricanes causing massive destruction in the USA, droughts around the world, massive fires that have destroyed thousands of homes, and killed hundreds of people. Also some scientist are saying we are in a major extinction event not see for 60 million years, all because of human impact on the environment.

LEFT VIEW:

- When humans temperate change from average 36 degrees to 38 degrees there is a problem imagine if the world warms by 2 degrees
- In 20 years there is going to be sea rises and coastal areas will be affected
- Need to do something now
- The next generations is going to be affected
- This natural disasters that just occurred is because of global warming
- It's the richer people who used more resources

RIGHT VIEW:

- Global warming is a scam
- It's not happening
- Green government have been elected on over-exaggerating the climate to suit their policy party
- If another country does not contribute or sign to improve the environment then why should we
- We shouldn't compensate the poorer nation

LEFT & RIGHT CIRCLE:

We need to the protect the environment / by this date the world will be underwater / vote for us we can fix it / Global warming is a hoax.

MIDDLE-ISM SOLUTION:

1. Need a worldwide concessions once and for all.

2. A Split between the environment and global warming. Its 2 different topics. Focus on looking after the environment than global warming will become easy. Politicians has got involved into the global warming where it shouldn't. The environment is everyone responsible government, companies and individual. It should be a "earth right" to look after the planet because according to some people where you believe in the ice age (science) or the great Noah floods (Bible and Quran) there is no planet like earth in the universal. We all live on the planet. All 193 nations should met their environment targets regardless of third world, developing, develope or rich & poor. 500 years ago its was to explore the new world but now there is no where else to go we can't get this wrong. Space settlement is still hundreds of years away.

3. Ignore the local greens party overexertion and predictions of the future to the environment, and push for 1 environmental policy world-wide. Individually, community and business if they are able should recycle, update new technology,.............. for their business, home and community.

4. Animals extinction should be the responsibility of every nation and monitored by the united nation. Animal extinction usually occurs to habitat loss and poaching. All should be done to save the animals that can be saved. This program can be easy be measured. Occasionally we know some animals cannot reproduce due to finding mates over a large area or no longer able to survive against superior competition.......

MIDDLE-ISM SAYING:

- By focus on the environment for the next 20 years by doing this right this will get a better and cleaner environment for the next 100 years.

MIDDLE-ISM VISION DRAWING:

KIDS ENJOYING THE ENVIRONMENT